Hardy and Half Hardy Annuals

By

R. Irwin Lynch

British Library Cataloguing-in-Publication Data
A catalogue record for this book is available from the
British Library

A Short History of Gardening

Gardening is the practice of growing and cultivating plants as part of horticulture more broadly. In most domestic gardens, there are two main sets of plants; 'ornamental plants', grown for their flowers, foliage or overall appearance – and 'useful plants' such as root vegetables, leaf vegetables, fruits and herbs, grown for consumption or other uses. For many people, gardening is an incredibly relaxing and rewarding pastime, ranging from caring for large fruit orchards to residential yards including lawns, foundation plantings or flora in simple containers. Gardening is separated from farming or forestry more broadly in that it tends to be much more labour-intensive; involving *active participation* in the growing of plants.

Home-gardening has an incredibly long history, rooted in the 'forest gardening' practices of prehistoric times. In the gradual process of families improving their immediate environment, useful tree and vine species were identified, protected and improved whilst undesirable species were eliminated. Eventually foreign species were also selected and incorporated into the 'gardens.' It was only after the emergence of the first civilisations that wealthy individuals began to create gardens for aesthetic purposes. Egyptian tomb paintings from around 1500 BC provide some of the earliest physical evidence of ornamental horticulture and landscape design; depicting lotus ponds surrounded by symmetrical rows of acacias and palms. A notable example of an ancient ornamental garden was the 'Hanging Gardens of Babylon' – one of the Seven Wonders of the Ancient World.

Ancient Rome had dozens of great gardens, and Roman estates tended to be laid out with hedges and vines and contained a wide variety of flowers – acanthus, cornflowers, crocus, cyclamen, hyacinth, iris, ivy, lavender, lilies, myrtle, narcissus, poppy, rosemary and violets as well as statues and sculptures. Flower beds were also popular in the courtyards of rich Romans. The Middle Ages represented a period of decline for gardens with aesthetic purposes however. After the fall of Rome gardening was done with the purpose of growing **medicinal herbs** and/or decorating church **altars**. It was mostly monasteries that carried on the tradition of garden design and horticultural techniques during the medieval period in Europe. By the late thirteenth century, rich Europeans began to grow gardens for leisure as well as for medicinal herbs and vegetables. They generally surrounded them with walls – hence, the 'walled garden.'

These gardens advanced by the sixteenth and seventeenth centuries into symmetrical, proportioned and balanced designs with a more classical appearance. Gardens in the renaissance were adorned with sculptures (in a nod to Roman heritage), topiary and fountains. These fountains often contained 'water jokes' – hidden cascades which suddenly soaked visitors. The most famous fountains of this kind were found in the Villa d'Este (1550-1572) at Tivoli near Rome. By the late seventeenth century, European gardeners had started planting new flowers such as tulips, marigolds and sunflowers.

These highly complex designs, largely created by the aristocracy slowly gave way to the individual gardener however – and this is where this book comes in! Cottage Gardens first emerged during the Elizabethan times, originally created by poorer workers to provide themselves with food and herbs, with flowers planted amongst them for decoration. Farm workers were generally provided with cottages set in a small garden—about an acre—where they could grow food, keep pigs, chickens and often bees; the latter necessitating the planting of decorative pollen flora. By Elizabethan times there was more prosperity, and thus more room to grow flowers. Most of the early cottage garden flowers would have had practical uses though —violets were spread on the floor (for their pleasant scent and keeping out vermin); **calendulas** and **primroses** were both attractive and used in cooking. Others, such as **sweet william** and **hollyhocks** were grown entirely for their beauty.

Here lies the roots of today's home-gardener; further influenced by the 'new style' in eighteenth century England which replaced the more formal, symmetrical **'Garden à la française'**. Such gardens, close to works of art, were often inspired by paintings in the classical style of landscapes by Claude Lorraine and Nicolas Poussin. The work of Lancelot 'Capability' Brown, described as 'England's greatest gardener' was particularly influential. We hope that the reader is inspired by this book, and the long and varied history of gardening itself, to experiment with some home-gardening of their own. Enjoy.

HARDY AND HALF-HARDY ANNUALS
Soil—Sowing the Seeds—Staking—Varieties.

Fig. 159.—A Bowl of Asters

HARDY AND HALF-HARDY ANNUALS

The exact meaning of the term annual as applied to cultivated plants is that the life of the plant is limited to a period of twelve months in which it grows from seeds, flowers, and in its turn produces seeds and then dies.

Some plants, which are treated in the garden as annuals, are naturally either perennials or biennials. Conditions of cultivation determine, however, their term of existence.

SOIL

Annuals should be sown in a light rather than a heavy soil, although such strong-rooting subjects as Sweet Pea, Tropæolum, Lupin, Convolvulus, and others are more at home in a somewhat heavy soil. It should be deeply dug and well pulverized, the roots of many annuals travelling much deeper in the ground than is generally supposed. It should also be rich, in order that there may be a vigorous growth and a fine and continuous display of bloom. Annuals are frequently starved through being grown in poor, untilled soil, and this poverty of appearance is augmented when the plants are allowed to grow much too thickly, as is frequently the case.

SOWING THE SEEDS

The time to sow annuals in the open air is from the middle of March until the end of May, when the soil is warm and quick germination may be looked for. Many of the hardier kinds do extremely well and flower much earlier if sown in late autumn. Self-sown annuals indeed are evidence of this. For very small seeds the soil upon which they are sown should be as fine as possible, indeed it is well to have a specially-prepared fine compost for them. A general rule in sowing is to cover the seed grains with some compost to the depth of their diameter, whether they be large or small; and in the case of the smallest seeds, gently pressing the soil about them when sown.

As the seedlings appear above the soil, and if the weather be dry, they should be watered overhead with a fine rose watering-pot. Bright sunshine and a dry surface will otherwise destroy many plants. Thinning-out is absolutely necessary in most cases, however careful the sower may have been in distributing the seeds; and this operation is done with the least harm to the remaining plants when the soil is moist. Annuals as a rule are of a much more branching habit than is generally supposed, but when this is prevented by crowding they are cramped and starved. The thinning should be gradual, so that it may be possible to transplant some of the seedlings to other vacant spots.

STAKING

Some of the taller growing annuals need support, which can be easily afforded by placing a few twigs about them. This support tends to increased robustness of growth, with consequent greater profuseness of bloom. Climbing plants, such as Sweet Pea, Convolvulus, Thunbergia, Tropæolum, &c., need taller supports.

The soil on which annuals are growing should be kept loose and free from weeds. It should also be regularly and well watered during times of drought; not merely moistening the surface, but soaking the soil.

Annuals are now much more appreciated than formerly, and numerous plants that used to be kept up from cuttings are now grown as annuals. This is an advantage and the result is often much the best. Annuals have a great advantage inasmuch that charming effects can be speedily secured at a moderate outlay. Some of them have not a prolonged season of bloom, but this may be extended by making several sowings successively. This is not always necessary, and a garden filled wholly with annuals can be made both interesting and enjoyable.

ACROCLINIUM ROSEUM (fig. 160).—One of the prettiest of the "Everlasting" Flowers. It forms shapely tufts about a foot high, and flowers freely and continuously during the summer, the colour of the flowers being bright-pink. If the flowers are cut when quite fresh and dried in the sun they retain most of their colour, and are useful for indoor decoration in winter. There are rose-coloured, white, single, and double varieties. The seeds should be sown in March, where the plants are to remain.

ADONIS.—This genus supplies two hardy annuals, viz. A. æstivalis, the Flos Adonis of seed catalogues, a somewhat dwarf form, with feathery leaves and crimson blossoms; and A. autumnalis, which, like the foregoing, has the common name of Pheasant's Eye or Red Morocco. The flowers are blood-red with a dark centre.

AGERATUM.—Several useful summer-bedding plants have been derived from A. mexicanum, a somewhat tall-growing species, now displaced by varieties of compact, bushy, free-blooming habit. By many they are propagated from cuttings with other bedding plants, but they are also treated as annuals, seeds being sown in early spring in a gentle heat, and the plants gradually hardened off for service in the flower-beds. Imperial Dwarf, blue-flowered, and a white variety of the same; Little Dorrit, and a white-blossomed counterpart; Tall Blue; and Tall White are very suitable for large beds.

ALONSOA.—A genus comprising six species, the best of which is A. Warscewiczii, of somewhat shrubby growth, and when cultivated in pots and protected it is sub-perennial. It grows to a height of 12 inches, bearing in July attractive small orange-red flowers from seeds sown in light soil in March. Albiflora, white; linifolia, scarlet; Compound Scarlet; and Compact Pink are also worth growing.

ALYSSUM MARITIMUM.—Sweet Alyssum, a native of Britain, in its garden form is a small annual of cushiony habit, bearing in summer and autumn numerous erect crowded umbels of small star-shaped white fragrant flowers. A useful plant

Fig. 160.—Acroclinium roseum

for edgings to borders, or to cover the soil in small beds. It is worth a place in the rockery, and we have seen it thriving on old walls. Easily raised from seeds. It is also known as Kœniga maritima.

AMARANTUS.—The several annual species are easily grown and very effective. A. melancholicus, if sown on good soil and allowed plenty of room, grows to a height of a yard or more, and produces large tail-like flower-heads. A. caudatus, well known as Love-lies-bleeding, and its forms are effective. A. hypochondriacus or Prince's Feather is also good; A. speciosus (pyramidalis) has erect flower-heads. These may be sown in the open border in early spring. There are several others, remarkable for the rich variegation of their leaves, viz. A. tricolor, as effective as a Coleus, but requiring to be raised in heat and planted out in May; other forms of it are bicolor, rubra, *splendens,* and *salicifolius,* also worth growing for their leaves.

ANAGALLIS.—Several charming annuals of garden origin have been obtained from *A. grandiflora* and *A. liniflora;* chief among them are *cœrulea,* blue; Eugenie, light-blue and white; Napoleon III, crimson. Seeds can be sown in light soil in a sunny position in the open air.

ANTIRRHINUM.—All the splendid varieties obtained during recent years, varying from white to pink, orange, scarlet, red, and yellow, which now come nearly true from seed, may best be treated for summer bedding as half-hardy Annuals. To flower from July to September they should be sown in February or March, shifting to pans or boxes and planting out after the spring bedders have been removed.

ARGEMONE.—Two species of this Poppy-like genus—*A. grandiflora* (fig. 161), white, and *A. mexicana,* light-yellow—are worth growing in the herbaceous border, as they are attractive both in leaf and flower. They grow to a height of from 18 inches to 2 feet, and flower continuously in summer. Seeds may be sown in the open ground in March.

ARNEBIA CORNUTA, growing about 2 feet high, is an ally of the perennial Prophet-flower, and like it has yellow flowers with an almost black spot on each petal, which disappears as the flower grows old. It is an attractive plant and likes a warm situation.

ASPERULA AZUREA SETOSA, related to the Common Woodruff, is very effective when grown in

Fig. 161.—Argemone grandiflora

a fairly light, rich soil, attaining a height of 1 foot, and bearing freely pale-blue flowers.

BARTONIA AUREA, with its large golden-yellow flowers, is a most showy plant when well treated,

Fig. 162.—Brachycoma iberidifolia

growing to a height of about a foot, of bushy habit, and flowering profusely in any good garden soil.

BRACHYCOMA IBERIDIFOLIA (fig. 162).—The Swan River Daisy, of which there are blue, rose, and white varieties. Snow Star is a new white variety. They form charming tufts a foot high, flowering in summer in an open sunny position. The seeds should be sown in a gentle hot-bed, and transplanted to the open in June.

BROWALLIA ELATA.—An elegant, loose-growing plant from Peru, of which there are several improved varieties. They are best treated as biennials, sowing the seeds in July, wintering them in a greenhouse, and planting in the open in early summer. *B. grandiflora,* from Colombia, and *B. Roezli,* from the Rocky Mountains, are also grown from seeds. *B. speciosa major* produces large blue flowers, and is cultivated as a greenhouse perennial to bloom in winter and spring.

CACALIA (EMILIA) COCCINEA is a pretty Composite, with brilliant orange-crimson flowers borne in clusters on erect stems a foot and a half high, springing from a rosette of ovate, stalked leaves, those on the stems being sessile. The var. *aurantiaca,* with orange-coloured flowers, is also charming.

CALANDRINIA.—Annual species of this genus are *C. discolor,* rose and yellow; *C. grandiflora,* pink; *C. Menziesii* (*speciosa*), purple crimson; and the Peruvian *C. umbellata,* which is practically a biennial. Allied to the Portulacas. Sow the seeds on somewhat open, sunny spots where they are to flower, as the corollas expand only in bright sunshine, when they are very showy.

CALENDULA OFFICINALIS, the Pot Marigold, and its varieties are useful in the flower-garden in summer. Orange King and Lemon Queen, both double-flowered, are worth a place in any garden.

They grow rapidly, and bloom profusely and continuously. As soon as the flowers fade, the heads should be picked off to encourage the production of bloom. There are several single varieties ranging from pale-buff to orange, but the double forms are most effective.

CALLIRHOË.—Allied to the Mallows. Forms of C. digitata and C. involucrata, commonly known as Poppy-Mallows, although classed as perennials, are more frequently treated as annuals, seeds being sown in spring in the open, or else in pans and transplanted. They grow and flower best in a light sandy soil.

CALLISTEPHUS CHINENSIS (fig. 163), the China Aster.—This popular garden annual is roughly divided into two sections—the quilled and the

Fig. 163.—Callistephus chinensis

flat-petalled. The former, known as the German Aster, has by means of selection been brought to a high state of perfection; the base of the flower-head has one or two circles of flat ray florets, and a symmetrical central cushion of quilled florets. They are taller and more branched than the flat-petalled forms, and are much esteemed for exhibition purposes; also excellent for cutting. The flat-petalled section includes a variety of strains with large handsome flower-heads, and suitable for a variety of purposes. Ostrich Plume Asters are very fine and resemble certain Japanese Chrysanthemums. The Victoria Asters are among the finest for exhibition. The Bedding Asters are dwarf and compact, suitable for summer bedding. The Comet group is one of the best for cutting purposes. The Crown-flowered Aster is also flat-petalled; the distinguishing feature of this group is that the blossoms are two-coloured, a disc of white forming the centre, surrounded by a marginal zone of some bright shade of rose, crimson, purple, &c. What is known as Truffaut's Pæony-flowered Aster has the florets incurved, and when well grown they

are almost hemispherical. As high culture is required to produce fine blooms this sort is not so much grown for the purpose as formerly, but all Asters require good soil and liberal treatment. Single Asters, which are now obtainable in various colours, are exceedingly valuable for cutting. The Ray Asters produce immense flower-heads with long slender, quilled florets, very telling in floral decorations. Seeds should be sown in prepared beds in a frame or house, or in pans or boxes, in March and April, in a compost of finely-sifted loam, leaf-mould, and sand, which should be well watered before the seeds are sown. If glass can be laid over the tops of the pans germination is much hastened. Should the surface become dry, water is best administered by placing the pans, &c., in a vessel of water where it can gradually soak to the surface, instead of sprinkling overhead. As soon as the seedlings are large enough, they are pricked into boxes or a prepared bed in a frame, and hardened off for planting in the open ground. Some of the dwarf-growing Bouquet and other Asters are admirably adapted for pot culture, and are employed in this way for the decoration of the greenhouse. Good results are obtained by potting up plants in bloom, and much trouble is saved. Well-tilled and rich soil is indispensable for the production of a fine head of bloom in the open air. The flower-heads may be thinned for size, as in the case of Chrysanthemums.

CAMPANULA.—This genus comprises annuals, biennials, and perennials. C. macrostyla is a very distinct and ornamental annual, about a foot high, of loose growth, producing large purple, pink, or white flowers, with dark reticulations of striking character.

CELOSIA CRISTATA, the Cockscomb, is a favourite annual for pot culture, but it may also be used for beds in summer. It is grown in this way in Paris, the plants having been planted out in frames, then moved with balls of soil to the final position. C. plumosa, in various colours, is used for bedding in some London parks. Seeds must be sown in heat in February or March.

CENTAUREA.—A large genus of annuals or biennials, the most useful of which is the blue Corn-flower of the fields, C. Cyanus, improved by cultivation and selection. In addition to blue there are white, grey, pink, and rose colours, and also a double form. They are tall, and will thrive in any out-of-the-way position. The blue-flowered forms are largely cultivated for cutting purposes. C. moschata includes the blue and white Sweet Sultan, and C. suaveolens, the Yellow Sultan, all most useful for cutting purposes. They are also serviceable when grown in pots for the conservatory in early summer. Improved varieties are " The Bride " and " Bridesmaid ", the former with white and the latter with yellow flowers. " The Bridegroom ", heliotrope in colour, is also good.

CENTRANTHUS MACROSIPHON, an ally of the perennial Spur-Valerian, is an attractive plant with large heads of red flowers.

CHEIRANTHUS CHEIRI, the Wallflower, is usually biennial, but the kind known as Paris Market is really annual. Sown in March, the plants flower in summer, and on to the opening of the well-known sorts of spring. Yellow Phœnix makes a bright show throughout the winter. There is also a Brown Phœnix.

CHRYSANTHEMUM (fig. 164). — The annual species are numerous and very useful. C. coro-

narium, with its numerous large single white, yellow-eyed flowers, erect in habit, and 2½ feet high; the double white and double varieties are of great value for cutting purposes. *C. carinatum* (tricolor) and its several varieties are very handsome and single-flowered. There is a double-flowered strain of this, larger and more varied in colour than the double forms of *coronarium*, but not nearly so symmetrical. *C. multicaule* is a dwarf, single-flowered yellow variety. *C. segetum*, the yellow Corn-flower of the fields, is represented by improved garden forms. The seeds of annual Chrysanthemums may be sown

Fig. 164.—Annual Chrysanthemums

in the open air in thoroughly good soil, and the plants thinned out to admit of ample development. Within the last few years a race of single-flowered forms have been obtained by crossing *C. coronarium* and *C. carinatum*.

CLARKIA.—Numerous varieties of *C. elegans* and *C. pulchella* that have originated in gardens. They comprise tall and dwarf, double- and single-flowered forms, with white, pink, red, or variegated flowers. The doubles, raised in recent years, are very striking and are among the very finest of border annuals. The best are: Firefly, vivid rose crimson; Scarlet Beauty; Snowball; and Purple Prince. They make a good show in beds.

CLINTONIA (*Downingia*).—A genus of Californian annuals allied to Campanula. Two species, *C. pulchella*, blue, and *C. elegans*, white to purple, are cultivated both as border plants and in pots for the conservatory. The seeds are sown in February in a little warmth, and the

seedlings intended for the open air are transferred to the beds in May. In warm situations the seeds may be sown out-of-doors in April. They are useful for front positions on the herbaceous border.

COLLINSIA BICOLOR is a favourite; it grows to a height of 1½ feet, and has purple and white flowers. *C. grandiflora*, pink and blue; *C. violacea*, white and violet; *C. candidissima*, pure white; and *C. verna*, blue and white, are all worth growing. The seeds of the last-named should be sown as soon as ripe. They do well in any good garden soil, and are excellent pot annuals.

COREOPSIS (*Calliopsis*) includes some fine showy annuals as well as perennials. *C. bicolor*, with yellow and brown flowers, is the progenitor of most of the varieties grown. They are rather tall, reaching a height of 3 feet. *C. Drummondii* is of dwarfer growth, and produces bright-yellow blossoms. *C. tinctoria*, Beauty and Crimson King, the former chiefly yellow and the latter dark crimson, are splendid for the border. *C. Atkinsoniana* has yellow and brown flowers, excellent for cutting. *C. grandiflora* is a biennial, but if sown in March in warmth will flower the same season; it grows to a height of 2½ feet and produces large golden-yellow flowers. A dwarf-growing annual race has also been obtained.

COSMOS BIPINNATUS (Mexican Aster).—With graceful foliage and beautiful flowers, useful for cutting as well as for garden decoration, the several colours of this fine plant should be grown in every garden. There are crimson, orange-red, rose, and white forms, varying in height from 3½ to 4 or 5 feet. The late American forms should be avoided, but these are not now likely to be met with. It is recommended to raise in heat in March, and plant out in warm sunny position when danger of frost is over, but sowings out-of-doors where intended to flower have been perfectly successful. *C. sulphureus*, with golden-yellow flowers 2 feet high, is a fine border plant. It is distinct as a species from the last and is also native of Mexico.

CUPHEA MINIATA, with scarlet flowers, is distinct and beautiful. *C. Zimapani* may also be grown; it is of rich plum-colour but ruins *C. miniata* by crossing with it, and they should not be grown near one another.

DELPHINIUM. — The annual Larkspurs are divided into two sections—the tall and the dwarf. Some of the former, the Stock-flowered in particular, grow to the height of 3 feet, while the Dwarf Rocket, a form of *D. Ajacis*, scarcely exceed a foot. Large and finely-formed blossoms are produced in handsome spikes; and the colours vary considerably. The tall varieties of *D. Consolida* branch freely, Emperor being one of the finest. The seeds should be sown in pans, and the young plants transplanted in May in the case of heavy soils; but the seeds can be sown in the open when the soil is light. Rosy Scarlet is valuable for beds and for cutting.

DIANTHUS CHINENSIS (fig. 165).—The Indian Pink, both single and double forms, and its improved variety *Heddewigii*, are easily grown, and well repay good cultivation. In *Heddewigii* the flowers are considerably enlarged, and in the form known as *laciniatus* the petals are fringed. A few fine varieties, such as Brilliant, Crimson Belle, and Eastern Queen, generally come true from seed. The doubles are very fine. Treated generously, the plants flower all through the summer up to November in a favourable season. A section known as *Imperialis* is taller, with smaller flowers, and is useful for cutting.

Fig. 165.—Indian Pink

DIMORPHOTHECA AURANTIACA (fig. 166), the Namaqualand Daisy, is one of the best of annuals. It has flowers of a soft orange colour with black central ring and grows about 9 inches high. *D. pluvialis* is the well-known Cape Marigold, with white Marguerite-like flowers, the under-

side of the petals a rich maroon. It grows about 1 foot high. Between these two hybrids have been raised which vary in colour from pure white to salmon-orange and yellow. There are some doubles; they approach *D. aurantiaca*. *D. sinuata* is similar to *D. aurantiaca* but of light-chamois colour with bluish disk and reverse of petals purple-red.

ERYSIMUM PEROFSKIANUM (Hedge Mustard) is one of the commonest of hardy annuals, and produces plentifully its trusses of deep-orange blossoms. A dwarf form known as *E. arkansanum* has bright-yellow blossoms; the seeds of both can be sown in the open ground in spring. The former is sometimes sown in autumn, with the result that the plants bloom earlier.

ESCHSCHOLTZIA.—Showy easily grown annuals. *E. californica* is represented in gardens by numerous varieties with yellow or orange flowers. One called *maritima* is yellow-spotted with deep-orange. Mandarin, dark bronzy-orange; Ruby King, deep ruby; Mikado, orange crimson; and Rose Cardinal, pale rosy-pink, are worth special mention. The usual practice is to sow the seeds in the open ground in spring, to bloom in the summer. They are, however, much finer when sown in autumn, and as they stand the winter well they grow to a large size and require ample space. In a sandy soil they root deeply and bloom magnificently.

GAILLARDIA.—The plants of this genus are really perennial, but they are said to be a success when treated as half-hardy annuals.

GILIA.—A large genus of hardy plants, chiefly annuals. The most popular is *G. tricolor*, 2 feet high, with lavender and white purple-eyed flowers. *G. nivalis* is snow-white with an orange eye, and is delicately scented, having an attraction for bees. *G. coronopifolia*, with scarlet-crimson flowers, is a very handsome plant. It is often biennial in behaviour, but succeeds when treated as a half-hardy annual, sowing the seeds in January. All others require to be grown as hardy annuals. *G. capitata*, with mauve flowers, should be included. They do best in a fairly light soil.

Fig. 166.—Dimorphotheca aurantiaca

Fig. 167.—Helianthus cucumerifolius

GODETIA.—Closely allied to Œnothera, indeed it is included in that genus by botanists. *G. Whitneyi*, introduced from California in 1870, and its numerous garden progeny, now so widely grown, are very effective free-flowering annuals, with large heads of cup-shaped blossoms, which, when cut, retain their beauty for a considerable time. Duchess of Albany, Sunset, Bridesmaid, Scarlet Queen, Lady Albemarle, The Bride, and Gloriosa, rich orange-crimson, are all delightful varieties. The double Crimson, Rose, and Mauve are splendid. They do well in any good garden soil, either when sown in the open, or when raised under glass and planted outside in spring. Height 12 to 18 inches.

GRAMMANTHES GENTIANOIDES.—This is a charming annual for the rockery and may be sown where it might not be convenient to plant a perennial. It has orange-red shaded flowers and grows about 3 inches high. It belongs to the Crassula family and is native of South Africa. It must be classed as half-hardy.

GYPSOPHILA ELEGANS is a useful annual 18 inches high, bearing feathery lilac blossoms, useful for bouquets. It does best in a light and fairly dry soil. The variety Rosy Gem is of bright carmine-rose colour, White Pearl is snow-white.

HELIANTHUS (Sunflower).—A very large genus which includes some remarkably fine annuals, double and single, large and small flowered; some very tall in growth, others quite dwarf. The giant single, *H. annuus*, with its enormous heads, will reach a height of 8 to 10 feet, while the dwarf sorts scarcely exceed a yard in height. Of these, *H. cucumerifolius* (fig. 167), with small yellow heads and dark centres, may be especially recommended. *H. argophyllus*, with silvery foliage and medium-sized yellow flowers with dark centre and growing about 5 feet high, is also

good. There are various fine varieties of *H. annuus*, and the New Red, growing about 6 feet high, is one of the most remarkable. The doubles should not be overlooked. They are admirably adapted for massing in shrubberies and the mixed border. Seeds are best sown in April, in a little warmth, the young plants to be placed out in the open when 6 inches high, after being hardened off. Or the seeds may be dibbled in the open ground in good rich soil in May. There are now miniature forms which grow into dense bushes and produce their flowers in great abundance.

HELICHRYSUM MONSTROSUM (fig. 168).—One of the most popular of Everlasting Flowers. It grows to a height of from 2 to 3 feet, and flowers profusely if planted in a sunny position. Colour, chiefly reddish-bronze and yellow. If cut with a good length of stem when about half-expanded, and tied in bunches and hung up head-downwards in a cool dry place, they dry and retain their form and colour and are useful for winter decoration.

HELIPTERUM.—The Australian *Acroclinium roseum* and its varieties, together with *Rhodanthe Manglesi*, are now included in this genus, and are classed as hardy summer annuals. *H. Sandfordii* has bright-yellow flowers. Seeds are sown

Fig. 168.—Helichrysum monstrosum

in March in a gentle heat, and transplanted to the open ground when it is safe to do so. They may also be sown in the open ground with good prospect of success.

HIBISCUS TRIONUM is a handsome hardy annual, 2 feet or so high, with numerous large rounded blossoms, their colour a delicate primrose with a deep-violet centre.

HUMULUS JAPONICUS and its variety *variegatus* are annual Japanese Hops, and are most useful summer creepers for covering fences and walls quickly with their ample and handsome foliage. The variegated form comes true from seeds.

IBERIS.—The Candytufts are popular by reason of their hardihood, and crimson, lilac, and white flowers. The best are Snow Queen, white; Giant-flowered White; Rose Cardinal, rose; Kermesina, crimson; and Rosy Dawn, flowers white shading to rose. The seeds should be sown in fine soil, and the plants well thinned to allow room for development, then they branch freely and flower for a considerable time.

IONOPSIDIUM ACAULE is a lovely Crucifer, not more than 2 inches high, with a profusion of violet-coloured flowers. It will grow on any border, but in character is suitable for rock-work. While never a weed, it may be relied upon almost to maintain itself by self-sown seeds.

IMPATIENS BALSAMINA (The Balsam).—The fine strains of this useful annual seem to have disappeared from cultivation, but they are worth recovering. The seeds germinate quickly if sown on a brisk bottom heat, when they should be removed to a cooler temperature. They may be sown in pots, pans, or boxes of light soil, and if strong plants are wanted the seeds should be pricked singly into the soil, sufficiently wide apart to admit of the plants being lifted with soil attaching to their roots and potted. They require rich soil, and if to bloom as pot specimens they should be grown cool with ample ventilation and moisture. Liquid manure may be given as they come into bloom. Balsams do remarkably well in an open border, in a sunny position and good soil. The Camellia-flowered and the Rose-flowered are the finest strains. *I. glandulifera* and *I. Roylei*, both sturdy Himalayan annuals, 3 to 5 feet high, are useful for covering unsightly places or for the stream side, but they sometimes become weeds and are not easily kept within bounds.

IPOMŒA.—The best of the species available for out-of-door culture is *I. purpurea* in its numerous forms, popularly known as *Convolvulus major*, *C. minor* (fig. 169), &c. Others that may be grown in the warmer parts of this country are *I. coccinea*, *I. Learii*, and *I. rubro-cœrulea*. It is usual to give these greenhouse culture, but if planted out on a rich border they grow freely, and are often very floriferous during summer. *I. Bona-Nox*, the Good-Night flower, may also be grown against a sunny warm wall; its large white blossoms open at night. *I. versicolor* (*Mina lobata*) is an attractive and free-flowering half-hardy annual, most useful for covering a warm wall during summer. The plants should be raised under glass, hardened off and planted out at the end of May.

KAULFUSSIA AMELLOIDES, a native of South Africa, is an ornamental hardy Daisy-like annual, blue-flowered with a yellow disc. There are garden varieties of it with white, rose, yellow, carmine, &c., flowers. The variety *Kermesina* is dark-red. The seeds may be sown out-of-doors in ordinary soil about the middle of April; or on a hot-bed earlier in the year and transplanted.

KOCHIA TRICHOPHYLLA, the "Summer Cypress", a native of China, growing about 3 feet, is one of the most charming foliage plants, pale-green in summer, but turning to dark-red in autumn. It forms a dense symmetrical bush, the leaves very narrow.

LAVATERA TRIMESTRIS and L. SPLENDENS are beautiful and showy hardy Mallow-like annuals, of tall growth, and producing large and striking rose-coloured or white flowers. Seeds germinate freely when sown in the open ground, but the soil should be rich and holding.

LAYIA (OXYURA) CHRYSANTHEMOIDES (ELEGANS), a North American plant with yellow composite flowers and a pure-white variety of it, are useful

Fig. 169.—Convolvulus minor

dwarf annuals, about a foot in height, flowering freely, and remaining for some weeks in bloom.

LEPTOSIPHON, in gardens, is represented by a group of dwarf-growing annuals, raised by the intercrossing of two or three species. They are very compact in habit, and extremely free, but they do not last a great time in blossom. On warm and sunny spots and in a light rich soil they are showy and useful as edgings to plants of taller growth. *L. roseus*, *L. androsacens*, and *L. aureus* are particularly attractive.

LEPTOSYNE MARITIMA.—A perennial, formerly included in Coreopsis; grows to a height of 1½ feet, and produces large lemon-yellow Marguerite-like flowers, on long stalks; is also useful as an annual. *L. Stillmani* is not unlike the last-named, but it flowers earlier, usually within a few weeks from the time of sowing. They prefer a light soil in a sunny position, and should be raised from seeds grown in a little warmth in February, planting out in May.

LIMNATHES DOUGLASII, from California, of dwarf and rather spreading growth, forms dense tufts of yellow and white blossoms in early spring.

Fig. 170.—Linum grandiflorum

Years ago this plant was grown from seeds sown in late summer, and played an important part in spring gardening, being hardy, and coming into bloom with the Daisy and Wallflower. Bee-keepers should grow it about the hives.

LINARIA comprises a large number of species mainly from the Northern Hemisphere. The hardy annuals are the Portuguese L. bipartita, L. maroccana from Morocco, and several others which have been intercrossed, and from them have sprung various forms bearing parti-coloured yellow, orange, crimson, and black blossoms. L. reticulata aureo-purpurea is especially pretty, and L. tristis has a charming character of its own. Being dwarf and free, they soon form a brilliant floral picture in the garden.

LINUM includes a few annuals, the North African L. grandiflorum (fig. 170), and its variety rubrum, being by far the best. The latter is known as the Scarlet Flax. It prefers light soil and full sunshine, growing to a height of 18 inches.

LOASA LATERITIA (L. AURANTIACA), though a half-hardy perennial, is so much employed as an annual that it may be included here. Its twining, free-flowering habit and large red blossoms make it a useful summer climber. Seeds sown in light sandy soil in May germinate readily; it is usual to raise them in heat and transplant to the open ground in May. The leaves sting, so that it require careful handling.

LOBELIA.—The South African L. Erinus has come to play a very important part in the flower-garden in summer. Numerous seedling varieties of it have originated in gardens; they are dwarf and compact, and very floriferous, and are largely employed for summer bedding. Their colours include various shades of blue, crimson, and purple, also white, the blue-flowered sorts being most esteemed. They come fairly true from seeds, but the white kinds have a tendency to revert to the type. Usually, however, when employed for bedding purposes, they are propagated from cuttings, which strike freely in a little warmth.

Seeds should be sown in pans in a warm house or frame, where they quickly germinate. As soon as the second pair of leaves are developed the seedlings may be transplanted to other boxes, and grown on until large enough to be hardened off before planting them in the open. Some of the most popular varieties are Blue Stone, Crystal Palace compacta, Emperor William, &c., blue; Royal Purple, purple; White Gem, White Lady, and White Perfection, white. Names change, but from any good catalogue a reliable selection may be made.

LUPINUS.—It would be difficult to trace the parentage of the garden Lupins; probably, however, most of them have sprung from L. hirsutus, L. luteus, L. mutabilis, L. nanus, and L. polyphyllus, the latter a perennial. They are free-blooming generally, but their flowers are of short duration. The prettiest of the dwarf sorts are the forms of the blue-flowered L. nanus. The seeds of this are much smaller than those of other species and varieties. A selection would include L. Hartwegi, pure white, blue and white, or blue; L. hybridus albo- and atro-coccineus and subcarnosus, and L. Menziesii, yellow. The seeds should be sown in the border in April.

LYCHNIS CŒLI ROSA is a valuable annual both for pots and the open ground. It grows from 1 to 2 feet high, bearing flowers from white to crimson. There is a carmine dwarf 6 inches

Fig. 171.—Annual Lupins

high. The old garden name for this is Viscaria oculata.

MALCOLMIA MARITIMA (Virginian Stock).—One of the prettiest of hardy annuals, being dwarf, profuse, and quick to bloom, and doing well in almost any soil and position, even in gardens in some of the most densely-populated districts of London, where but very few annuals will thrive.

Fig. 172.—Ten-week Stock

There are varieties with rose, crimson, white, and yellow flowers. It will sow itself where it has flowered, come up, and bloom the same season. Few annuals so well deserve a place in the garden.

MALOPE TRIFIDA GRANDIFLORA, a native of Southern Spain, is one of the most showy hardy annuals, with large crimson flowers. There are rose, white, and striped forms of it, all very ornamental, and growing freely from seeds. The average height is about 15 inches.

MATTHIOLA (Stock).—A popular genus which in some form or other can be found in every garden, and in cottage gardens superior strains of the Brompton Stock often form the chief ornament. The various forms of Ten-week Stocks (fig. 172) are from M. annua, which was introduced from Southern Europe in 1731. The Wallflower Stock (fig. 173), the Brompton and Queen strains, treated as biennials, are said to be from M. incana, a native of West Europe, including the Isle of Wight. The Wallflower-leaved Stocks have shining green smooth leaves, the others have soft and downy leaves of a glaucous tint. But the Wallflower foliage will appear among seedlings from downy-leaved strains. There are several other sections, viz. the Common Ten-week, which includes the Large-flowered, the Pyramidal, and the Giant Perfection. Ten-week Stocks have been greatly improved, especially in the matter of white varieties. The Intermediate Stocks, scarlet, white, and purple, which are treated as biennials, are thought to be forms of the Ten-week, changed somewhat by selection. They are valuable for pots, sown in March for Autumn flowering. The East Lothian Intermediate Stocks represent a very fine Scotch strain, modified by climate. These are largely

employed for garden decoration in summer. The Brompton and the Queen types are distinguished by differences in the foliage, and the colour of their seeds. Large double-flowered crimson, purple, and white forms of the Brompton type are also grown, but they do not breed true from seeds. M. bicornis is the Night-scented Stock. It has lilac flowers with exquisite perfume.

Seeds of Stocks germinate freely when new and good; the best seed-beds are pans or shallow boxes, filled with a sandy compost, sowing the seeds thinly. Light and air are essential to a robust growth. When large enough the seedlings may be pricked off into a bed prepared in a cold frame kept a little close and shaded for a time, and then assisted to develop as lustily as possible. Incautious watering will sometimes cause the seedlings to damp off close to the soil. They are impatient of watering overhead. To do Stocks full justice they should be planted out in rich soil, to encourage them to develop not only their main stem, but also their side branches to the best advantage.

MESEMBRYANTHEMUM (Fig-Marigold).—A very large genus of herbaceous plants, chiefly South African. Several of them are annuals which thrive in the open air in summer in this country. The best are M. pyropeum (fig. 174) (M. tricolor), which form neat compact tufts 6 inches high, spreading freely over the ground and flowering profusely in sunny weather, the flowers being Daisy-like, purple, rose, and white. M. pomeridianum has large fleshy leaves and Marigold-like yellow flowers 3 inches across. M. crystallinum, the Ice Plant, deserves a place because of the interesting character of its leaves, which are covered with crystal-like pustules of ice-like appearance. The seeds of these should be sown where they are to flower, except that M. crystallinum may be sown under glass as it transplants

Fig. 173.—Matthiola annua

easily. They must have a sunny position, and if fairly dry so much the better.

MIMULUS (Monkey Flower).—During the past twenty years the Mimulus has been improved by crossing M. luteus and M. cupreus, the hybrids being called M. maculosus, with flowers mostly

Fig. 174.—Mesembryanthemum pyropeum

pale-yellow, heavily spotted and blotched with various tints. The seeds should be sown thinly in March in a pan of very finely sifted soil. As soon as the little plants will bear it they should be transplanted into pans or boxes and grown on until they are ready to be planted outside. They may also be cultivated in pots, in a frame, as they make a showy display and bloom freely and continuously. They seed freely, and the varieties come fairly true from seed. As the root-stock is perennial, they may be propagated by division, but seedlings produce the finest blossoms.

MIRABILIS JALAPA (Marvel of Peru), although a perennial, is generally grown as an annual. The seeds are sown in warmth in spring, and the seedlings planted out early in June, when they bloom profusely until late in the autumn. *M. longiflora*, the long-tubed Marvel of Peru, is very variable in the colours of its flowers; there are varieties with variegated leaves, also a dwarf or Tom Thumb section.

MYOSOTIS (Forget-me-not).—This genus includes several which are treated as annuals, viz. *M. alpestris*, blue, and its varieties white and sky-blue; *M. dissitiflora*, a biennial which is annually raised from seeds; and *M. sylvatica* and its varieties. Royal Blue, Star of Love (blue), and others are excellent. Ruth Fisher, with brilliant light-blue flowers, and Argentina, its white counterpart, are two of the best. The two latter somewhat nearly approach each other, but the former is finer, while differing somewhat in growth and in the character of the seeds. *M. alpestris* is frequently cultivated in pots. Plants of *M. dissitiflora* can be divided, but they are best when raised from seeds sown in July.

NEMESIA STRUMOSA (fig. 175), introduced by Messrs. Sutton & Sons, a beautiful annual from

Fig. 175.—Hybrid Nemesia (Sutton)

the Cape, produces varieties of differing shades of colour—white, pale-yellow, crimson, &c., and these in various combinations. The plant attains a height of 12 to 15 inches. The seeds should be sown in spring, somewhat thickly. They are most effective when massed and pinching is said to be of great value. If grown under glass the seeds may be sown at any time of the year; thus treated, the flowers come larger and better in colour. *N. floribunda* and its variety *compacta* are pretty little low-growing summer-flowering annuals, with white and yellow fragrant flowers. Beautiful hybrids have been raised with *N. strumosa.* Nemesias sown in September are excellent for winter flowering.

are freely and continuously produced. Hybrids of *N. affinis* with *N. forgetiana*, a red flowered species, raised by Messrs. Sander of St. Albans and called *N. Sanderæ* (fig. 176) are very fine. They range in colour from white, pink, red, to blue-purple. *N. sylvestris* is a beautiful fragrant white-flowered species of recent introduction, which has become highly popular on account of its robust stature, large leaves, and numerous flowers produced in dense panicles, and remaining expanded throughout the day. The large-leaved forms of the Common Tobacco, *N. Tabacum*, are striking objects in the sub-tropical garden, and in various sheltered spots. The seeds should be sown in March under glass, and the seedlings

Fig. 176.—Nicotiana Sanderæ at Kew: bed 12 feet wide, flowers crimson

NEMOPHILA.—Useful dwarf hardy annuals, natives of North America. They are easily cultivated and free-flowering. The best-known and prettiest is the blue *N. insignis*, of which there are several varieties, such as the white, the margined, purple-and-white, and the purplish-rose. Another pretty species is *N. maculata*; the lobes of its large saucer-shaped blossoms have each a dark-purple spot or blotch. Its seeds are larger and different in colour from those of *N. insignis*. *N. Menziesii (atomaria)* is distinct, and there are several varieties of it. If the seeds be sown in autumn and the plants kept through the winter, they bloom much more finely in spring than when sown in spring to flower in summer.

NICOTIANA.—*N. affinis* is a most popular and fragrant annual, thriving in small and confined plots and villa gardens. Its height is about 3 feet, and the long-tubed fragrant white blossoms

transplanted to the open in favourable weather about the end of May.

NIGELLA (Fennel Flower).—*N. damascena* is sometimes known as the Devil-in-the-bush; it has both pale-blue and white flowers, as well as double- varieties. *N. hispanica*, Love-in-a-mist, is represented by white and purple forms; the blue and white, known as Miss Jekyll, are the best for garden cultivation; the average height of the plant is 18 inches. Seeds may be sown in the open ground in March and April.

NOLANA.—Trailing, compact, Convolvulus-like annuals, of which *N. grandiflora* and *N. prostrata* are sometimes grown. They form cushion-like tufts of tongue-shaped leaves, and saucer-shaped white and blue flowers; seeds may be sown in the open ground in spring.

NYCTERINIA is represented by *N. capensis*, white, and sweet-scented; and *N. selaginoides*, of dwarf tufted growth, with lilac-coloured flowers. They are well adapted for culture in pots. The seeds may be sown in heat, but they do perfectly well sown where the plants are to flower. Natives of South Africa.

ŒNOTHERA (Evening Primrose) includes a few showy annuals, chief among them being Œ. *acaulis*, dwarf in growth, with leaves in a rosette, and bearing large white blossoms; Œ. *bistorta Veitchii*, yellow, with slight crimson blotches, 1 foot; Œ. *rosea*, rose-coloured; Œ. *Drummondii*, yellow, and its varieties tall and dwarf; Œ. *odorata*, yellow and fragrant, and others. They all grow rampantly in any garden soil, and are most effective in the evening. In some gardens they are naturalized, coming up promiscuously like weeds. Their near allies, the Godetias, are powerful rivals to them as far as use in the flower-garden is concerned. Œ. *biennis* is a handsome biennial, which may be grown as an annual by sowing the seeds in autumn. It is 3 to 5 feet high, with large bright-yellow flowers. Œ. *triloba* (*rhizocarpa*) is a hardy annual of dwarf growth, with large showy yellow flowers.

OMPHALODES LINIFOLIA (Venus's Navelwort) is a silvery-foliaged hardy annual growing to a height of nearly 9 inches, and bearing white flowers.

OXALIS ROSEA, in pink and white flowers, is a very desirable hardy annual, and it is good for pots.

PAPAVER (Poppy) includes many brilliant annuals, some of mixed parentage, and difficult to fix botanically. Shirley Poppies are improved forms of P. *Rhœas*, which have developed many beautiful tints and combinations of colours. They produce the finest blossoms when they are sown in the open in late summer where they are to flower. P. *glaucum*, the Tulip Poppy, with crimson flowers and whitish leaves, is very showy. P. *pavoninum*, the Peacock Poppy, is represented in gardens by named varieties. P. *umbrosum* appears to be a dwarf form of P. *Rhœas*. P. *somniferum*, the Opium Poppy, has produced many varieties, double and single; some entire-petalled, others with laciniated margins, but the duration of the flowering period of these is short. P. *Rhœas* and its allies are better, because they continue in flower longer, especially if the decaying blossoms be kept picked off. The Shirley Poppies (fig. 177) raised by Mr. Wilks deserve to be grown in every garden; a blue form has been raised in America. The double forms are known as Ranunculus Poppies.

PETUNIA.—A most useful addition to half-hardy annuals has been developed from P. *violacea*, previously known only as a greenhouse plant, and grown along with Heliotrope, &c., for summer bedding. They like a sunny position and a light well-drained soil. The colours of the flowers are varied and pleasing, whilst the habit of the plants is all that could be desired. Countess of Ellesmere, of beautiful rose colour, formerly grown from cuttings for bedding, can be raised with numerous other forms quite easily and even better from seed. The seeds should be sown in heat in February, and the seedlings, when large enough, should be transplanted singly into small pots to be planted out in borders, &c., towards the end of May.

PHACELIA CAMPANULARIA has bright-blue bell-shaped flowers which are highly attractive. It is an excellent plant for sowing over ground containing bulbs at rest. The seeds can be sown in the open in March, and the plants, which

reach a height of 6 to 9 inches, come into bloom early and continue to flower till autumn. P. *Whitlavia*, a Californian annual from which some fine varieties have been obtained, particularly *grandiflora*, violet, and *gloxinoides*, blue with a white throat. P. *tanacetifolia* is quite distinct from the others; it grows about 3 feet high, has violet-coloured flowers which are much visited by bees. They flower freely, the colours being intensified by cultivation in rich soil.

PHLOX DRUMMONDII (fig. 178) may be said to have taken the place of the Verbena in the flower-garden, as it has at many provincial flower-shows. The Continental florists have done much to

Fig. 177.—Shirley Poppies

improve the strain, the large-flowered varieties being really superb. The variety *grandiflora* in its various forms is beautiful. It is best to sow the seeds in heat and transplant to open ground in May.

PLATYSTEMON CALIFORNICUS, the Californian Poppy, is a showy dwarf hardy annual, bearing bright lemon-coloured flowers, and growing to a foot in height.

PORTULACA, popularly termed the Sun Plant, is an improved form of the Brazilian P. *grandiflora*. Of dwarf tufted growth, and bearing saucer-shaped corollas of various brilliant hues; there are double-flowered forms also. They do best on a warm sunny border in a light sandy soil. The seeds can be sown in the open in light soil, otherwise in boxes, and transplanted in May.

RESEDA ODORATA (Mignonette) is one of the most fragrant of hardy annuals. When first introduced from North Africa the blossoms were

Fig. 178.—Phlox Drummondii

yellowish-white, but by cultivation and selection they have nearly approached white on the one hand, and yellow, orange, and red on the other. The quality of the flowers is very much a question of selection. Only by saving seeds from the very finest can the strains be maintained. It is largely grown in pots for market, the seeds being sown in September in the pots in which the plants are to bloom. Enormous specimens in standard and bush shapes were formerly grown for the temperate house at Kew, attained by sowing early and pinching out the flower spikes immediately on their appearance. Mignonette requires rich soil, with ample space for the individual plants to develop, and then the result is satisfactory. The varieties Bismarck and Matchet are the best of the reds, Cloth of Gold and Golden Queen among the yellows, and Parson's White among the whites.

RICINUS COMMUNIS, the Castor-oil Plant, and its varieties are worthy plants for borders or beds in summer. The most popular are *R. Gibsoni* with red leaves and *R. zanzibarensis* of stout habit and massive foliage. They are readily raised from seeds sown in heat in March, and put out in the open as pot plants when hardened off.

SALPIGLOSSIS.—The varieties of *S. sinuata*, a native of Chili, are varied and rich in colour. When well grown they average 2 feet in height, and they are both profuse and lasting in bloom. Seeds sown in the open ground in good soil in March produce plants which, if allowed ample room, will be full-grown and in flower by June. In colder parts of the country the seeds should be sown in a little heat. Seedlings do not transplant well, and if the seeds are sown in small pots to avoid damage to the roots so much the better. The dwarf varieties are better suited for small gardens.

SALVIA.—A large genus, which includes a few good annuals, viz. *S. carduacea*, lavender-blue,

and *S. Horminum*, the beauty of which is due to the bracts, most commonly deep purple, but pink and white in other forms. Forms of *S. splendens* can be used for beds the same year by early sowing in heat.

SANVITALIA PROCUMBENS is a useful dwarf Mexican annual, bearing small Sunflower-like blossoms, yellow, with a dark disc. A double form of it flowers freely until late in the autumn, and is an excellent edging plant.

SAPONARIA (Soapwort).—This genus is well known by two annual species *S. calabrica*, a procumbent plant 6 or 9 inches high with red flowers useful for border margins, and *S. vaccaria*, an upright plant with rose flowers, popular in Paris for cutting. It is made up into dense bunches and commonly sold in the flower markets. There are white varieties of both species. The seeds should be sown in the open in March.

SCABIOSA.—The popular annuals, or, as grown by some, biennials, of this genus are varieties of *S. atropurpurea*, a native of Southern Europe. They vary in height from 1½ to 3 feet, and also in the size, colour, and fulness of their flowers. If the seeds are sown in boxes under glass in March, the plants will be ready to put out in May. In warm situations they may be sown in the open ground. They also do well when treated as biennials, sowing the seeds in April and treating the plants to flower in the following year. Some prefer to sow the seeds in pans or boxes in August, and grow on the plants in cold frames to flower in a cold house in early spring. They are most useful, easily-grown plants.

SCHIZANTHUS.—The Butterfly- or Fringe-Flowers are varieties of *S. pinnatus* (fig. 179) and *S. retusus*. They are grown to flower in spring

Fig. 179.—Schizanthus pinnatus

and early summer by sowing the seeds thinly in large pots in August and September and growing on the plants all the winter in a frame or greenhouse. Thus treated they form large bushes, a yard high, covered with elegant, many-coloured flowers, and are excellent for the conservatory. The forms of *S. pinnatus* are the best for pots. The strain known as *Wisetonensis* is dwarf and compact, but is less graceful. If to be grown outside, the seeds should be sown in April where the plants are to flower.

SCHIZOPETALON.—Walkeri is a pretty white annual of medium growth, the flowers of which are pleasantly fragrant in the evening. It is usual to raise the seeds in pots in a compost made up of loam, peat, and sand, planting the seedlings out in the border in May.

SEDUM CÆRULEUM.—A charming little half-hardy annual with pale-blue flowers. It looks best on a rockery.

SENECIO ELEGANS.—The Purple Jacobea is a useful free-flowering, hardy South African annual, growing in the form of compact bushes 1½ feet high. It is much employed for bedding purposes in summer. There are several varieties, with flowers varying from crimson to purple, white, rose, &c. There is a dwarf strain, *nana*, and there are forms with double flowers. Seeds may be sown in a moderate heat, and grown on into size, hardening the plants in a cold frame preparatory to planting out in a sandy soil. The blossoms are produced from July to October.

SILENE (Catch-fly).—There are two useful annual species of Silene, viz. *S. Armeria*, a loose erect grower 18 inches high, with numerous bright-rose flowers; *S. pendula*, 1 foot high, and its dwarf variety, *compacta*, both dense plants with crowded heads of carmine flowers in single and double forms, very free-flowering, and particularly serviceable in early spring. Empress of India, crimson, and Snow King, are good for beds; *ruberrima* also makes a fine show. There is a golden-leaved form. Seeds can be sown in the open ground in March and April for summer blooming, and in August for a spring display.

SPECULARIA (Venus's Looking-glass).—There are six annual species in this genus, which is closely allied to Campanula, the best-known being *S. Speculum* and its several varieties. The seeds should be sown in early spring in a sunny position. The star-shaped, purplish flowers are borne in June.

STATICE (Sea-Lavender).—The annual species of this genus are *S. Bonduelli*, golden-yellow, a foot high; *S. spicata*, rose-purple; and *S. Suworowi*, rose. These are worth growing in borders, as they flower freely and all through the summer, if raised under glass in early spring and planted in a sunny position outside in May. *S. sinuata* (fig. 180) has large flowers and varies in colour from pale yellow to deep mauve. It is a good pot plant. The flowers may be cut and dried to be used as Everlastings.

TAGETES (French and African Marigolds).—These are represented by two distinct types, viz. the strong-growing tall yellow African *T. erecta*, and the dwarf Mexican *T. patula* which has yellow flowers, striped with bright maroon. High character in both sections is maintained only by selection and good cultivation. The seeds are sown in heat, and the plants hardened off and planted out in the open at the end of May or early in June. A dwarf form of the Mexican *T. signata*, named *pumila*, is one of the most per-

sistent of the summer annuals. A single form of *T. patula*, named Legion of Honour, has dark florets broadly edged with yellow; Etoile d'Or is also good. A double dwarf form, known as *aurea floribunda*, is useful as a summer bedding plant. Single French strains are obtainable.

THUNBERGIA.—The annual species of this genus are not now so popular as they were. *T. alata* and its varieties, with white or yellow dark-eyed flowers, are charming summer climbers and trailers. The seeds should be sown in pots under glass, and the seedlings planted out in the open in warm sunny spots. They are also useful for furnishing vases.

Fig. 180.—Statice sinuata

TROPÆOLUM (Nasturtium or Winter-Cress).—The many form of *T. majus* are among the most free-flowering of annuals, whether dwarf or trailers. In rich soil they make vigorous growth, and continue in bloom till late in the year. Grown in poorer ground they flower with greater freedom, but the floral display is not so prolonged. The dwarf or Tom-Thumb section is a sport from *T. majus*, and by means of selection some most useful bedding varieties have been obtained. A selection may be made from any good seed catalogue. Some of the forms are useful for winter effect in greenhouses. Variegated-leaved forms of both tall and dwarf may be obtained. The seeds may be sown in the open in late spring, or in warmth, and transplanted. To keep any type of variety true to character, rigid selection is necessary. *T. peregrinum*, the Canary Creeper, with yellow flowers, is distinct and beautiful. From the popular name it is sometimes called *T. canariense*, though it is native of Peru and Mexico.

URSINEA PULCHRA.—A pretty little annual composite from Mexico, also known as *Sphenogyne speciosa*. It forms Daisy-like tufts of short stems from which spring the slender, erect flower-stems, a foot high, bearing single heads of yellow, dark-eyed flowers. There are several colour-forms of it, viz. *aurea*, *purpurea*, &c. The seeds may be sown in the border in autumn, where the plants grow and mature through the winter, to flower in April and May.

Fig. 181.—Verbena hybrida

VENIDIUM CALENDULACEUM is a somewhat prostrate-growing annual, having bright, clear, yellow flowers greatly resembling those of a single Pot-Marigold. It is very attractive, growing best on a warm, sunny border, in light soil.

VERBENA (fig. 181).—There is reason to believe that several species were utilized many years ago for the production of our garden Verbenas. They are now mainly employed as bedding plants, being raised from seeds sown in heat in early spring, as they quickly germinate in light, rich soil. They are potted off or transplanted into boxes, hardened off to be placed in beds and borders, where they grow very rapidly and soon flower, continuing in bloom until quite late in the summer. Although not now much valued

as a florist's flower, a few named varieties are still cultivated in pots, and increased by means of cuttings. Ellen Willmott, of beautiful salmon colour with white eye, comes fairly true from seed.

VISCARIA. See *Lychnis*.

XERANTHEMUM ANNUUM and its varieties, single and double flowered, form a group of useful and interesting Everlastings, the seeds of which can be sown in the open ground, in light, rich soil, where the plants are to bloom. The colours are purple, white, rose, &c. For preserving, the flowers should be cut with stems when about half expanded, and allowed to dry in a cool place.

ZEA MAYS (Indian Corn or Maize) and its variegated forms are good for subtropical beds, and are very easily raised from seed to be planted out when danger from frost is over.

ZINNIA.—There was a time not very remote when only the single form of *Z. elegans* was found in gardens—of somewhat tall and branching habit, and with very showy flowers. In course of time a double form appeared, and, by careful breeding and selection, the flowers are now large, full, very handsome, and varied in colour. Seeds are sown in a little warmth in spring, the plants grown on, and gradually hardened off for planting in the open. During the seedling stage they should not be starved or receive a check, or they will not bloom well. They are best grown in pots to be planted out without root disturbance. The soil should be deep and rich. The plants form handsome bushes and are prolific of bloom. *Z. Haageana* has both single and double flowers, but it is not so popular as the older race. There is a splendid giant strain of good height that should be grown. There are also Pompons. All the varieties remain in flower for a considerable time.

The decorative value of some Annual Grasses is now recognized. They are exceedingly graceful and charming plants for borders, and when cut they may be used either while living or when dried with good effect in floral arrangements. They are all quite easy to cultivate. The following is a good selection: *Agrostis laxiflora*; *A. nebulosa* (Cloud Grasses); *Avena sterilis* (Animated Oat); *Briza maxima* (Quaking Grass); *Eragrostis elegans* (Love Grass); *Hordeum jubatum* (Squirrel - tail Grass); *Lagurus oratus* (Hare's-tail Grass); *Lamarckia aurea*; *Panicum capillare*; *Setaria macroseta*. All grasses for drying should be gathered before the seeds ripen.

Lightning Source UK Ltd.
Milton Keynes UK
UKHW012028250921
391190UK00001B/93

9 781446 523650